Why Buy This Book?

If buying a car is in any way mysterious to you, you need this book! You may be vulnerable to sales and marketing techniques that you're not even aware of. If you feel buying a car is a crapshoot, this book is for you. Or if you just don't trust those damn car people, this book is *definitely* for you.

I have read, and I continue to read, a great many books, articles, and brochures on the subject of car buying. Not one of them even comes close to helping you understand what's involved in buying a car the way this book does.

- **Q.** Why do you suppose the questions about car buying persist?
- **A.** Because they haven't been answered . . . until now, that is!

This book takes away the mystery from buying a car (or any other vehicle). Read this book, and you'll be able to spot every scam from a mile away. Best of all, you'll walk away from the dealership a winner every time!

The *Only* Way to Buy a Car

David J. Hanley

RoundHouse Books

1994

Book design and editing: Barbara Bell Pitnof
Cover design: Sarah H. Bennett
Cover photograph: Robert W. Allen

RoundHouse Books
P.O. Box 866
West Side Station
Worcester, MA 01602

© 1994 by David J. Hanley

All rights reserved. No part of this book may be reproduced or transmitted in any form or by any means, electronic or mechanical, including photocopying, recording, or by any information storage and retrieval system, without prior written permission from the publisher. Contact the publisher for information on foreign rights.

This book is sold as is, without warranty of any kind, either express or implied, respecting the contents of this book, including but not limited to implied warranties for the book's quality, performance, merchantability, or fitness for any particular purpose. Neither the author, RoundHouse Books, nor its dealers or distributors shall be liable to the purchaser or any other person or entity with respect to any liability, loss, or damage caused or alleged to be caused directly or indirectly by this book.

This book can be an invaluable text and teaching tool for courses in consumer education and those that seek to develop market-wise students. Contact the publisher for information on group or volume sales.

Library of Congress Catalog Card Number: 94-69594
ISBN 0-9644155-0-X

Printed in the United States of America

Acknowledgments

There are a few people I'd like to recognize for their contributions to this book. All of you please stand up and take a bow when your name is mentioned:

- **Barbara Bell Pitnof.** This book owes its readability and fine appearance almost entirely to Barbara. Along with having incredible skills with words, Barbara is a great humanitarian. It's an honor to know her.
- **Katherine Hanley, my wife, and my stepson, John Michael Cusick.** Thank you both for your unwavering support and for tolerating my inattention while I worked on yet another project.
- **Don McEwen.** Don is a guy who has held about every imaginable position in the car business. Through his experience ranging from salesman to sales manager, F&I manager to dealership owner, to his present position, used-car manager with Lundgren Honda of Auburn, Massachusetts, Don has become an expert in all aspects of the automobile business. He also happens to be a straight shooter and he's quoted frequently throughout this book. His contribution was invaluable.
- **John Witte.** John has been a salesman and F&I manager and is presently sales manager at Lundgren Honda. He provided valuable assistance on the topic of vehicle leasing, covered in Chapter 5.

About the Organization of This Book

Some of you no doubt are more savvy about the business of buying a car or a truck than others. If you find you know the material in a certain section, you may want to read just the summary of important points I've included at the end of each chapter. I do encourage you to read each chapter in its entirety, though. You always can learn something new. Some of you may get the most from a book like this by skipping around. Feel free to do so. Although I've covered each important topic, it's not necessary for the chapters to be read in any special order.

Contents

	Introduction	3
1.	**I Know Exactly What You're Going Through** A sobering introduction to the retail automobile business	5
2.	**Now Matter How You Slice It: What Your Trade-In Is Really Worth**	15
3.	**Financing, or "How Much Do You Want Your Monthly Payments to Be?"** What you need to know before you even think about financing your car at a dealership	29
4.	**Aftershock . . . uh, I Mean . . . Aftersell** An inside look at a quiet but big money maker for car dealerships	43
5.	**To Lease or Not to Lease** An easy decision once you've finished this chapter	53
6.	**D-Day or Mayday?** Putting it all together for your day at the dealership	65

Contents

7. How to Buy a Car   **81**

    Car-Buying Worksheet   **87**

    Glossary of CarSpeak   **89**

The *Only* Way to Buy a Car

Introduction

Watching television not long ago, I came upon a show about a new customer service training program taking place at Chrysler Corporation. From the front office all the way down to the dealerships, the goal of the program is to educate all Chrysler personnel in the proper treatment of customers. Not a bad idea, I thought.

The show was mildly interesting, but one comment made by a Chrysler vice president was nothing short of amazing. Roughly, it went like this: "There was a study done once where most people responded they would rather have a root canal than have to go out and buy a new car!" A *root canal!* Can you believe it? Now, I knew shopping for a car was bad, but I guess I didn't realize just how bad.

It's great that all of these MBAs and genius executives are finally starting to realize what the customer has known all along: Treat the customer badly, and eventually the customer will treat you badly, or, at the very least, with indifference. Hey, what comes around goes around.

I find it amusing that companies are spending millions on programs to teach their employees something easily reduced to just a few words: Treat customers with respect. They are your bread and butter. Treat customers fairly. Which means, no matter how tempting, don't rip customers off.

See how easy it is? Maybe they should make me an ex-

Introduction

ecutive at a Big Three car company. For a few thousand dollars, I could have sent a personal note with the same message to every Chrysler employee and saved the company millions.

So what's the point of all this? The point is *they are still missing the point!* Car manufacturers and dealerships take note: Until the price of a car and accessories is no longer a negotiable item, customers will continue to be ripped off and treated badly. Until salespeople are no longer paid commissions based on profits, all the incentives to lie, cheat, deceive, mislead, and otherwise treat customers poorly will remain. If salespeople must be paid commissions, pay them a volume-based commission, not a per-vehicle profit-based commission. And give them an added incentive for getting high marks from customers. The same goes for service. Stop paying your service writers (the people who write the repair orders when you go to have your car serviced) commissions. Talk about a formula for disaster.

You can wait for all of these touchy-feely training programs to trickle down to the dealership and transform the salespeople into Girl Scouts and Boy Scouts, but don't hold your breath. Most car dealerships' reputations stink, and they deserve it. They're not misunderstood; they're not maligned. It's taken years of customer abuse for this fear and loathing of dealerships to become a permanent part of the American psyche. I'll bet car salespeople are the least trusted people on earth.

Read this book. It's your best defense against every rotten sales trick ever invented. Read this book, you'll never have to worry about being ripped off by a car dealership again. I promise.

1

I Know Exactly What You're Going Through

It's true. I've been on both sides of the car-buying fence. Buyer and seller. Inflictee and inflictor.

My job as a car salesperson was a kind of fluke. One of my friends was making fairly good money selling cars, and money was something I definitely needed at the time.

Lo and behold, in no time I was making three times what I had made at any previous job. More important, I embarked on one of the most illuminating experiences of my young life.

But enough about me already. The pages that follow are intended to benefit you, the consumer — to level the very uneven playing field of the retail automobile business. If I can spare just one of you from falling prey to the scams that I myself perpetrated on many unsuspecting customers, then this effort will have been worthwhile.

This chapter is a general introduction to (a warning about) the car business before we move on to the real nitty-gritty of the actual deal. It's not my intention to put fear

The *Only* Way to Buy a Car

into your heart or cause you greater anxiety than you already have about stepping into a car dealership. No. The goal of this chapter, the goal of this book, is to give you the power to control the outcome of your next car purchase. The best way to do that is by helping you understand how dealerships everywhere operate and by showing you how to respond appropriately.

■ The Good, the Bad, and the Really Ugly

Let me begin by telling you something you may not be aware of: They're having a sale today at your local car dealership. Tomorrow too. And the next day. And the day after that. Don't think for a moment that you can buy a car for less money because it happens to be a certain day of the week or month. Don't believe the ads, the commercials, or the hype. It's pure fallacy. *You can buy the car you want, for the price you want, any day of the year.* If you don't believe this now, you will by the time you've finished this book.

Cars are a commodity. And that's good news for you, the consumer. Like conditions in the consumer electronics and personal computer markets, the automobile market is glutted with look-alikes, perform-alikes, and price-alikes. The sheer number of makes and models available and the "sameness" of their style and function make it difficult to distinguish among them.

So why is this sameness good? Well, maybe I should qualify that. For *most* people, the sameness is good. It's not so good if you're really big on style and you don't have a fortune to spend on a really stylish car. Why? Because it costs more and more these days to buy something that is truly unique. But it's great if you're like most of us who'd rather

I Know Exactly What You're Going Through

choose a vehicle for a number of more practical reasons, style included, those of us who'd rather not be at the mercy of a dealership simply because it sells a car we've been led to believe will make us look twenty years younger and twenty pounds lighter.

The fact that cars are so much alike only serves to increase competition in an already competitive market. Because the cars themselves are indistinguishable from one another, dealers and manufacturers must resort to other means to get your attention. This benefits the consumer by forcing dealers to compete on the basis of price.

But this book isn't about helping you *choose* a car. As they say, there's no accounting for taste. What this book *is* about is three things:

- Helping you understand exactly what takes place when you buy a vehicle
- Helping you understand exactly what you're paying or giving up for your new vehicle
- Helping to ensure that once you've figured out which vehicle you want, you'll be able to walk into a dealership and buy that vehicle without worrying about getting ripped off

In learning these things, I guarantee you'll save a minimum of $100 (hey, a hundred bucks is a hundred bucks) — an unbelievable return on your investment in this book. More likely, though, you'll save several hundred or even a thousand dollars or more if you just follow the guidelines in this book. Read on!

The *Only* Way to Buy a Car

■ Some Things to Consider Before You Go Shopping

Why is it shopping for a new vehicle has become one of America's least liked activities? After all, who doesn't enjoy getting something new? Especially something big, shiny, and expensive? Unfortunately, most of the joy of buying a new car has been stripped away by the bad experiences we've had at a dealership or the many horror stories we've been told by others. Sadly, I'm inclined to believe most of those stories.

The reasons car shopping has become so unpleasant are many. I think most of us understand that the car salesperson really is not there to *help* us in the true sense of the word. This may be why many of us are anxious when we have to look for a new car.

Sure, salespeople gladly give you an earful of facts and figures about all of the wonderful features offered with their car. However, this information is readily available from any number of brochures, magazines, and newspaper articles. And you have to question the objectivity of information when its source has a vested interest in having you buy one of their automobiles.

When it comes right down to it, the automobile salesperson is there for one purpose: to sell you a vehicle right then and there, and to sell it to you for as much money as possible. Now this statement may generate some backlash from car people, but show me one who really disagrees and I'll show you a liar. (And *that* statement is going to generate even more backlash!)

Salespeople are agents of the dealership. They are not in any way acting on your behalf. Now this may seem obvious, but you'd be surprised at the number of bright men

I Know Exactly What You're Going Through

and women who buddy up to the salespeople and treat them as though they were old friends. *Don't do it.* It will cost you in the end.

Another reason for the great level of discomfort we feel when car shopping is that many salespeople are very skillful at selling. It's their job to make you feel a sense of obligation to buy from them. Have you ever noticed how soon after entering a car dealership that you start to feel the pressure to buy, when you may have gone there only to shop around?

Beware. What may seem like nothing more than casual conversation with a salesperson is more likely a carefully controlled dialogue designed to uncover important information about your car-buying status. This information can include, among other things, which of their vehicles is best suited to you; what your general income level is; whether you are a potential finance customer (dealerships make big money on financing — more on that later); on which features to concentrate the sales effort; and, of course, which vehicle will yield the greatest profit to the dealership. This is what's known as "qualifying" you.

With this information the salesperson is trying to determine on which model and features to concentrate his or her selling efforts based on your financial ability to enter into a binding contract *right then and there!* It does the salesperson absolutely no good to get you excited about a luxury car if your income only allows you to drive a compact. Likewise, it is fruitless for the salesperson to be showing you around the lot if you are just there to drool over the new models. While you're drooling, he or she may miss other customers who have a pile of money burning a hole in their pockets!

The *Only* Way to Buy a Car

■ Low Tech Goes High Tech

Automobile dealers, like other retailers, have learned to take advantage of technology in an effort to improve their business. At a dealership where I once worked, salespeople were required to watch satellite-beamed sales-training programs on TV. These programs demonstrated the very latest in sales techniques that had been proved statistically to produce results. The whole process we go through when buying a car has been dissected and analyzed. The result of this technology is a systematic approach to car selling that leaves few stones unturned and is very unforgiving on the customer.

Please believe me when I tell you this: Each and every element of the sales process has been analyzed and reanalyzed, documented, and planned. You cannot surprise or outfox a well-trained salesperson, someone who's anticipated and prepared a response for everything you say.

Remember the salesperson's incentive: Almost all automobile salespeople are paid commissions calculated on the *profit* on their sales, not on the gross sales price as salespeople are in most industries. So giving you a good deal turns out to be a bad deal for them. Also studies have shown that a person who visits a dealership for the first time and doesn't buy in all likelihood won't make a second trip to the same dealership. More often than not, the person will buy a new car elsewhere. This may have more to do with subconscious factors related to the buying cycle than with any dissatisfaction with the dealership or its products.

Obviously salespeople have a lot of motivation to try to pressure you into buying a vehicle the very first time you step into their showroom.

For this book, I interviewed Don McEwen, the used-car

I Know Exactly What You're Going Through

manager at Lundgren Honda in Auburn, Massachusetts, and an expert in the automobile business. His comments clearly illustrate the reality of the salesperson/dealership advantage:

> The average car salesman negotiates more car deals in one day than a person does in their life. Yet, 90 percent of the people who come into the dealership feel they are armed to the teeth and ready to negotiate a salesman down to nothing. But they're wrong. Because there's an old saying in this business, "It's not the deal you get, it's the deal you think you get." And it's very important. Because, we'll make you feel like you got a good deal. Whatever you want.

You must remember these people are highly trained and put these skills to use for as many as sixty or seventy hours each week. A good salesperson can make $50,000, $60,000, or even $75,000 a year. An excellent salesperson can make over $100,000. Little wonder the person who buys a car once every three or four years is at a tremendous disadvantage when it comes time to negotiate at the dealership.

In fairness, there are some dealerships that pay their salespeople a straight salary or a combination of salary and commissions. Recently, you may have noticed the emergence of the "one-price" dealership. The car dealership where Don McEwen works is a one-price store, and he believes strongly in this arrangement:

> Our one-price and most one-price stores are developed from the Saturn model program. Saturn's

The *Only* Way to Buy a Car

one-price, it's sticker price, and it works. . . . We have to really price competitively because the other (Honda) dealers can undercut us . . . because they're not all one-price.

What they do here is decide how much money they need to make in order to make a profit and pay a commission and so forth, and also remain competitive. We hope that by offering good service and follow-up after the sale, and throughout the ownership of the car, we'll get the business of the customer.

But not all aspects of the one-price dealership accurately fit that description. As you will see in the coming pages, car dealerships sell a whole lot more than cars, and a one-price dealership is no exception.

There also are a very few dealerships whose policy it is to sell cars for a fixed number of dollars above the dealer invoice price. But be forewarned: The definition of *invoice* can differ widely from one place to the next. Most dealerships still use a commission-per-vehicle system to pay their help, so you should assume this is the case when you go shopping.

The buyer and the seller have completely different — make that conflicting — objectives. What this means is that you are trying to buy a vehicle for as little as possible, while the salesperson and the dealership are trying to get you to pay as much as possible. It's no wonder that the experience of buying a car is so frightening. Were it not for the near absolute necessity of having a vehicle, I seriously doubt whether anyone would choose to set foot on a car lot. Little surprise, then, that some people these days pay a car broker to do their bidding for them.

I Know Exactly What You're Going Through

■ Beating the Odds

By now you should be starting to understand that from the dealer's point of view, the whole process of someone buying a new vehicle is a tightly controlled event. It is not just a series of random occurrences that ultimately conclude with a customer mysteriously (and happily, of course) acquiring the perfect car at the right price. This is what the car dealer might want you to believe, but it is rarely the case.

No. A trip to a car dealership more closely resembles a night at a casino, and you know who usually ends up winning at a casino. Each and every aspect of the process has been scrutinized and strategies have been developed, all for the dealership to come out ahead. That's why you have to have a strategy of your own. Fight fire with fire. You have to be able to see where a salesperson is trying to lead you and to take control of the situation.

Car dealerships are the *worst* places to shop for a car, at least while you are in the early stages of trying to decide what you want. Do your homework elsewhere. Read magazines. If you must, run in and grab a brochure. But don't linger. If you need to see a car in person, wander around a dealership lot when the place is closed. Talk to people who already own the car you want. You know what you want and need from a car. A salesperson can't tell you any more about a car than magazines or a brochure can! In fact, they're inclined to tell you less. The less you know, the fewer things you can object to as the salesperson steadily leads you toward the purchase of a new vehicle.

Most people win or lose at a car dealership when they sit down to make a deal. Some lose even before. Later on we'll talk about what to expect from the moment you walk into a dealership and how you can control the situation

The *Only* Way to Buy a Car

from start to finish. Now, though, we're going to learn to master the most important element of car buying: how to make the deal and win, each and every time.

Chapter Summary

- That many of today's cars are styled alike and perform alike has increased competition among dealers and created a market ripe for negotiation.
- The dealership and the customer have conflicting objectives: The dealership wants the most money it can get for its products, while the customer wants to pay as little as possible. This is the fundamental reason that the process of buying a car is so uncomfortable. It's also the reason for all the gimmicks.
- Be wary of seemingly casual conversations with car salespeople. They are collecting information about you all the time, and they use that information to get you to buy.
- Not everything at one-price dealerships is one-price.
- Don't go to car dealerships in the early stages of car buying. You're just inviting trouble. Read magazines, newspapers, and the reports of consumer groups to narrow down your choices. Go to a dealership when it's closed to get a firsthand look at a car. Remember that salespeople are trained to try to sell you a car the first time you walk in the door.

2

No Matter How You Slice It: What Your Trade-In Is Really Worth

How many times have you gone to buy a car thinking you have a good idea of how much you'll have to pay, only to wind up completely confused after hearing all the talk about trade-ins, financing, rebates, down payments, and book values? What about the stickers, sometimes three or more, on the vehicle window, each showing a different price? Or why does the salesperson try to persuade you to lease when you really want to own the car? These things don't happen by accident. They are designed to confuse you and add profits to the dealer's pocket. Once again, remember the salesperson's motive: to get you to pay as much as possible for your vehicle.

In this chapter we talk about trade-ins. In the process, we begin to reduce a car deal to its most basic elements, to understand just what it is you are giving up in exchange for your new car. Be patient. This is the toughest chapter in

The *Only* Way to Buy a Car

the book. It's filled with terms and examples that may require more than one reading for you to understand them.

■ About Trade-Ins

For many people, the trade-in is the most confusing part of the car deal. In general, if you are able to sell your old vehicle privately you are much better off. Why? Because the dealer places a value on your trade-in equal only to what it believes it could sell it for immediately. This is what is known as the *wholesale* or *actual cash value (ACV)* of the car. Let's say that your car is worth $8,000 if sold privately or at a dealership. If the guidebooks tell the dealer that the ACV of the trade-in is $5,000, then your car is worth $5,000 to the dealer and that's all it's going to allow you toward the purchase of a new car. Period. Is that clear?

Now, a salesperson isn't likely to tell you this because the salesperson doesn't want you storming out of the showroom or squeezing his or her neck until his or her eyes pop out of their sockets. If you are able to sell your old car on your own, right from the start you'll be ahead by an amount close to the difference between the retail price of the car and the ACV — usually at least $1,000, but often $1,500 or more.

Let me try to explain why this is so. When a dealer accepts a vehicle in trade, it's not sure whether the car will be held for sale to another customer or will be sold to a third party (an auctioneer or a used-car dealer, for example). Sales to third parties typically are made at prices approximating wholesale or ACV.

Now, it costs a lot of money to keep cars in inventory, and sometimes a dealer needs to generate a cash flow or

No Matter How You Slice It

make room for more vehicles. So the dealer sells a group of cars — sort of a package deal — to a third party. When this happens, the dealer, to induce the buyer to accept some less desirable vehicles, may have to include in the package some cars it actually would like to keep for retail sale. For reasons that essentially have to do with accounting and bookkeeping, the dealer needs a consistent way of assigning value to trade-ins. Thus the concept of actual cash value.

Actual cash value is the highest price at which ordinary buyers would run to the dealership to buy the car if it was offered for sale at that price. It theoretically represents the highest price at which a dealer can convert a car *instantly* into cash.

In reality, the ACV figure usually comes from a guidebook of the most current selling prices at major dealer-only car auctions, with a little bit of judgment from the dealer thrown in. These guidebooks are published monthly or sometimes weekly. Chief among these "blue books" is the *Official Used Car Guide,* which is published by the National Automobile Dealers Association Used Car Guide Company (N.A.D.A.®).

Because the difference between the ACV and the retail price (the price for which the car would be sold to an individual) is usually not as great as the $3,000 in the example I gave a while back, the dealer can hide the difference by offering you what appears to be something close to retail for your trade-in. Some people call this an *overallowance;* but you're not really being overallowed anything.

What the dealer really is doing is absorbing the difference into the profit on the new car. So if the retail value of your used car is $1,500 greater than the ACV, and the dealer's got a $3,000 markup on the new car, the dealer just tells you it's giving you retail for the trade-in and

The *Only* Way to Buy a Car

reduces its profit by $1,500. After all, it's still got $1,500 to play with.

In other words, the dealer's going to reduce its profit on the new car to keep the value of the trade-in equal to the ACV on its books. However much short the wholesale value of your trade-in is from the retail price, the dealer's going to have to discount the new car by the same amount. This way the dealer gives you the impression that it's allowing you an amount close to the retail value for your trade-in.

By the way, this is a convenient way for the dealer to keep salespeoples' commissions down too. From the dealer's viewpoint, the trade-in is equal to cash in the amount of the ACV. Therefore, the lower the trade-in amount, the lower the total received for the new car and the lower the "book" profit on the car. Consequently, the lower the commission paid to the salesperson.

Let's try working through an example. Suppose you're considering a new vehicle, we'll call it a Lemming, with a sticker price of $18,500. Assume there is a $2,900 markup (profit) built into the sticker price. In other words, the dealer's cost is $2,900 less than the sticker price.

You want to trade in your three-year-old Silver Sliver toward the purchase of the Lemming. Because you've looked in the newspaper at the classified and dealers' ads, you know the going retail price for three-year-old Silver Slivers in good condition (just like yours, of course) is about $5,995. (It's amazing how prices always end in ninety-something, isn't it?) The dealer's blue book, on the other hand, shows the ACV for your particular Silver Sliver as $4,000. That's a difference of $1,995 between what you think you should get for your car and what the dealer is going to allow as payment toward a new car.

Now, how do you think you would react if the dealer of

No Matter How You Slice It

fered you just $4,000 for your precious Silver Sliver? You just might entertain the idea of performing the choke hold I described earlier. But all is not lost. Because there is a $2,900 markup in the price of the Lemming, the dealer can tell you something like this: "Well, we can give you the $5,995 in trade for the Sliver, and you'll have to give us another $12,505 in cash."

Scenario 1: *How the Dealer Wants You to See It*

Sticker price of the new Lemming	$ 18,500
Minus:	
Trade-in value of the Silver Sliver	− 5,995
Equals:	
Cash needed with trade for the new Lemming	$ 12,505

Now, I know this adds up to $18,500, the sticker price of the Lemming. But, on the books, the dealer's only receiving $12,505 in cash plus the $4,000 ACV of your Sliver, for a total of $16,505 for the new Lemming. Here's where the markup comes into play. Remember that there's a $2,900 markup on the Lemming. The dealer's cost is only $15,600 ($18,500 minus $2,900). So the dealer's still making a healthy (excessive in my book, and this *is* my book) $905 profit, and you walk away thinking you got a great deal!

Scenario 2: *How the Dealer Sees It*

Cost of the new Lemming	$ 15,600
Minus:	
ACV trade-in value of the Silver Sliver	− 4,000
Equals:	
Cash needed with trade-in to break even	$ 11,600

The *Only* Way to Buy a Car

From the dealer's standpoint, what really has taken place here is that you've traded in a car with an actual cash value of $4,000 — in essence $4,000 in cash — and have paid another $12,505 in cash (you may have taken as a car loan), for a total of $16,505. To some folks, giving the dealer a $905 profit may be acceptable. I look at it and see that you could have saved another $800 or more!

Scenario 3: *How the Dealer Figures Its Profit*

Cash paid toward the new Lemming	$ 12,505
Plus:	
ACV trade-in value of the Silver Sliver	+ 4,000
Equals:	
Total value given for the new Lemming	$ 16,505
Minus:	
Dealer's cost for the Lemming	– 15,600
Equals:	
Profit on the sale of the Lemming	$ 905

The smart shopper would look at the sale from the dealer's point of view (Scenario 2). Assuming you know the dealer's cost for the Lemming (and there are ways of finding out that I'll explain later), your thinking should go like this: "The dealer's cost for the Lemming is $15,600. Subtract the ACV of the Sliver ($4,000), which leaves $11,600 — the dealer's breakeven point, or cost. I'll offer $11,700 and my car to buy the Lemming right now."

That's right, you're offering the dealer $100 profit right now as opposed to the $905 you may have paid just so your feelings wouldn't be hurt hearing your Sliver is worth only $4,000. Granted, the dealer may turn around and sell your Sliver for $5,995 tomorrow, making itself a revolting $1,995 profit, but that's the price you pay for trading and at least

No Matter How You Slice It

the dealer got you only on one end of the deal. Using dealership accounting methods, you were able to limit the dealer's profit to $100 on the sale of the Lemming.

Let me confuse you a little more. Let's say you were on your toes and paid only $11,700 plus your Silver Sliver for your new Lemming. After all this fancy footwork, you still feel as though you've paid too much. Well, from the buyer's perspective, you really have. After all, you've given the dealer a trade-in that's worth $5,995 on the retail market and cash in the amount of $11,700 for a total of $17,695, not $15,700, which includes the $100 profit you thought you were offering. In a sense, you're right. This is why it really is better to sell your old car privately, as I suggested at the start of this discussion on trade-ins.

Had you been able to sell the Sliver for $5,995, you would have been able to apply that money and an additional $9,705 (not $11,700!) toward the purchase of the Lemming. This way, you would only have given up $15,700 ($5,995 plus $9,705) for the Lemming — a great deal for you and only $100 profit for the dealer!

"So," you say, "what makes you so sure the dealer would sell me the car for only $100 above cost?" Well, the amount may vary between $100 and $300. We'll talk about the reasons later, but one primary reason is that when you really are ready to make the deal, and I mean *ready* to sign the papers if you get your price, you have to say the magic words: "I'll buy the car right now *if* you're willing to meet my terms." These words produce wondrous results at a car dealership.

In Chapter 1, I mentioned the studies that show how people usually don't go back to a dealership for a second visit. And I also mentioned how the similarities in cars and the heavy competition among dealerships have forced

The *Only* Way to Buy a Car

dealers to lower their prices to remain competitive. Well, add these things up and you get a pretty good explanation of why dealers are willing to take as little as $100 profit or to just break even on the sale of a new car. If they can't make big profits on a small number of sales, it makes sense to take small profits on lots of sales. Besides, there are other ways for a dealer to make profits in addition to selling new vehicles.

There is another element that factors into a dealer's willingness to accept a small profit on the sale of a new car. Known as *hold-back*, this practice once was used only by domestic car dealerships. Today, however, some foreign car dealerships use the arrangement.

According to Don McEwen, *hold-back* means that when a dealer pays for a car, the manufacturer sets aside (holds back) an amount equal to 3 percent of the car's retail price. Car dealerships that use this system get back what amounts to a rebate equal to 3 percent directly from the manufacturer as each new car is sold. So even if a dealer is selling you a car at "invoice," it's still getting its 3 percent.

Don argues that hold-back helps dealers offset their *floor planning costs*, the interest they pay to finance their inventory of cars. (You didn't really think they owned all of those cars, did you?) That may very well be the case. However, the real effect of hold-back is that dealers do not really pay "invoice" for their cars.

The bottom line on trade-ins: Sell your car on your own if at all possible. It's better to have the money in hand than to have a car that represents an unknown value when you're trying to negotiate. You know the expression "A bird in the hand is worth two in the bush." If you do decide to trade, accept the fact that you are giving up the difference

No Matter How You Slice It

between the retail value of the car and the ACV. Think of your trade-in as the equivalent of cash in the amount of the ACV (but don't just accept the dealer's estimate of ACV as gospel). It will make things much clearer and limit the dealer's opportunities to razzle-dazzle you with confusing figures.

One more thing while we're on the subject of trade-ins. If you're still planning to trade in your car, absolutely positively make sure the car is clean and looking its best. Whether you're trading or selling, there is no more economical way to enhance the value of your car than to have it sparkling clean inside and out.

A note of caution if you do decide to sell your old car yourself. Some states require the seller of a used vehicle, whether a dealership or an individual, to provide certain warranties with that vehicle. Under certain circumstances this could backfire on the seller. Contact your state's Office of Consumer Affairs to find out what the warranty requirements are when you sell your car.

■ How to Determine the ACV for Your Car

There are several ways of determining the ACV of a vehicle. One is to use the dealer's method of choice, the blue book. The most readily available blue book is the *Official Used Car Guide* published by N.A.D.A. The actual book isn't blue at all, although its contents might make you blue.

This pocket-sized volume used to be carried by most bookstores and occasionally the book sections of some department stores. On a recent trip to my local bookstore, though, I discovered that the book was only available in the

The *Only* Way to Buy a Car

retail consumer edition, which lists the going retail prices for used cars. This definitely is *not* what you want.

I wonder why the dealer's edition is no longer available at the bookstore? Do you get the feeling somebody would prefer you not know what you're doing? When asked, my good friend Don McEwen responded, "I think your readers might be happy to know that they can check it [the dealer's edition] out of their local library."

Before you look for your information in the blue book, you should know that there are different editions — for example, there's a New England edition — for different parts of the country. Make sure the edition you're using corresponds to your geographical location. The *Official Used Car Guide* is published monthly, so make sure that you're using a current copy as well.

At first glance, the N.A.D.A. book (or any other blue book) can be very confusing. You are confronted with page upon page of numbers and dollar amounts, columns and rows, charts and conversion factors. Don't worry. Like everything else in the car business, it's relatively simple to get the information you're looking for. You just need to know where to look.

Let me preface this by explaining a little something about bankers and other lenders. Bear with me. Lenders always try to protect themselves, right? In the case of a mortgage (which is exactly what a car loan is), the only time a lender has loaned more money to the borrower than the property is worth is when the lender has made a serious error in judgment. The same holds true for vehicles. The lender wants to be able to recover its money as quickly as it can in the event the borrower stops paying on the loan.

With respect to a used car, then (in case I've lost you,

No Matter How You Slice It

we're talking about placing a value on your used car), doesn't it make sense that a lender would want to loan a car buyer only an amount of money it could recover immediately if the borrower stops paying? The key word here is *immediately*. Now does that ring a bell? The amount a lender will lend on a used car is the ACV! When you're looking up the ACV of your soon-to-be old car in the N.A.D.A. book, you want the figure given under the column heading "Av'g Loan," which means "Average Loan," or in car-lot lingo, ACV. One and the same.

Some other things to think about when you're using the blue book to find the ACV value for your car: Questions always come up concerning the options or features your car may have or the mileage for a car of that model year. Generally, the most important items considered by a dealer are the following:

- Is the car in clean, fair, or rough condition? (These are the classifications used in most blue books.)
- Does the car have an automatic transmission and air conditioning?
- Is the mileage what it should be? (For mileage adjustments, just round up or down to the nearest thousand miles. If the mileage is significantly, say 5 percent or more, over or under the average, adjust the value using the price per thousand miles given in the blue book.)
- Does the car have any special option packages that increased its original price by a substantial amount? By this, the book means a package that would move a car up in model designation. For example, going from a base model to a DX model, or going from a base model to say the Wild West version. These must be the manufacturer's distinctions, not the dealer's add-ons, and are not

The *Only* Way to Buy a Car

simply additional individual options like cruise control and tilt wheel.

The *Official Used Car Guide* is divided into three main categories: domestic cars, foreign cars, and trucks. Within each category, vehicles are listed alphabetically, first by manufacturer and then by model name. Just remember, the most important factors in determining the ACV are the ones I've listed above. Dealers generally do not add small amounts to the ACV for individual options such as power door locks or intermittent windshield wipers.

Another method of obtaining the ACV for your car is to visit a number of used-car dealers and ask them point blank how much they would pay you for your car today or tomorrow. Because they are in the business of selling vehicles at a profit, they certainly are not going to offer you retail price for your car. By going to several dealers, you'll be sure to eliminate the chance of one offer being too low or . . . ahem . . . too high. So you should come up with an average pretty close to the ACV.

One final method of determining the ACV of your car is to call the consumer loan department of your bank. The bank keeps a current copy of a blue book on hand for purposes of making loans. Be sure to say that you want the actual cash value, or average loan figure if the bank has the N.A.D.A. book, for your car. Any other number is useless.

The best method of determining ACV I suppose, would be to use a combination of all of these methods if you have the time.

No Matter How You Slice It

Chapter Summary

- Selling your old car on your own is always a better alternative than trading. When you trade, the dealer wants to make money both by selling your old car to someone else and by selling you a new car. Because of the need to have a consistent way of putting a value on used cars, the dealer always uses the actual cash value to assign an amount to a trade-in.
- The ACV theoretically is the price at which the dealer could sell the trade-in immediately. In reality, the ACV comes from any number of industry blue books in combination with the dealer's judgment. The best known blue book is the N.A.D.A. *Official Used Car Guide.* The value in the guide representing the ACV is the average loan figure. Other considerations in determining the ACV of a used car are its condition, mileage, type of transmission, air conditioning, and special option packages.
- When calculating how much you'll pay for your new car along with your trade, consider the trade-in to be worth cash in the exact amount of the ACV. This way you won't be confused by a dealer telling you it's giving you the retail price for your trade-in when, in fact, it's simply discounting the price of the new car to absorb the difference between the retail value and the ACV of your trade-in.
- If you're still planning to trade in your car, absolutely positively make sure the car is clean and looking its best. Whether you're trading or selling, there is no more economical way to increase the value of your car than to have it sparkling clean inside and out.
- If you plan to sell your car privately, just be sure you're aware of sellers' warranty obligations in your state.

3

Financing, or "How Much Do You Want Your Monthly Payments to Be?"

Don't answer that question! I repeat, do *not* answer that question! Before I explain why, let me tell you a little something about a dealership where I once worked.

This dealership was located in an almost rural town a good 20 miles from the nearest city. Everything about the place was "plain vanilla." No fancy storefront, just a showroom at least twenty-five years old, sporting worn green vinyl linoleum squares on the floor. It was barely big enough to hold five cars if you squeezed them in just right. Even the front lot was small, and most of it wasn't even paved. But there was nothing plain vanilla about the way this place operated.

From this unassuming little storefront rolled a steady stream of new and used vehicles in numbers good enough to rival most of the city dealerships 20 miles away. The most remarkable thing, however, was not that it sold as many vehicles as it did, but that of the four separate income-pro-

The *Only* Way to Buy a Car

ducing areas in the dealership — sales, service, finance, and auto body — the one that ranked second behind sales in total profits was finance. "So what," you say. The finance department consisted of one, count 'em, *one* person! This person was single-handedly able to generate enough income by selling loans, loan insurance, and various other postsale goodies to customers to earn himself a tidy salary in excess of $90,000. The best salesperson in the house was still $25,000 to $30,000 shy of that amount!

"How can this be?" you ask. It is mostly because so many unsuspecting customers answer the question, "How much do you want your monthly payments to be?"

In this chapter I'll explain enough about the financing of a vehicle to keep you out of trouble. And we'll take a brief look at rebates and other "incentives."

■ Financing

If you haven't noticed, I've got a habit of beginning these chapters with sweeping generalizations. Why change now? In general, you're better off not to finance your vehicle purchase at all. What I mean is, pay cash if you can. Now I know that's just not possible for most people, and that's why this chapter is here.

An automobile loan is simply a mortgage. And a mortgage is a loan in which the property purchased with the borrowed funds is pledged as collateral or security for the loan. In other words, if you don't pay the loan, the property can be taken away by the lender to recover its money.

Back in Chapter 1, I hinted briefly that car dealerships make a great deal of money by financing the vehicles they sell. Let me explain how it works.

Financing, or "How Much..."

When a dealership finances a car, it really is *selling* the loan money to the car buyer for another party. This concept of selling money is sometimes hard for people to grasp, but that's exactly what's taking place. The other party is usually a bank or one of many huge credit-granting institutions like GMAC or Ford Motor Credit. Now instinctively you know the dealership isn't merely doing this as a favor to these companies.

On any given day, the dealership contacts the various lenders it works with and is quoted an interest rate at which it (the dealership) could borrow money for purposes of making vehicle loans. This interest rate is known as the *buy rate*. The buy rate also happens to be less than the rate a customer will be charged to borrow the money. Do you see where this is going?

So let's suppose the buy rate for today is 6 percent. In comes our customer, Joe Beyer (bad, I know), who has happily agreed to purchase a new car. Because it's so convenient, Joe has decided to finance with the dealership as well. Now Joe has no idea what a buy rate is and really shouldn't care anyway. So when the dealership offers to finance the $10,000 he needs for five years at 8.75 percent, Joe's as happy as a clam.

And so is the dealership. For ten minutes' work, if you can call it that, the dealership has just picked up another $782.40 in profit. This amount is the difference between what the dealership *would* pay for the money, or the buy rate of 6 percent, and the 8.75 percent Joe is paying over the life of the loan. The total of Joe's payments of $206.37 over 60 months is $12,382.20. The total payments at the buy rate of 6 percent ($193.33) over those same 60 months would be $11,599.80.

The dealership is very soon sent a check for the differ-

The *Only* Way to Buy a Car

ence of $782.40 minus, say, 2 percent of that amount, and Joe makes his payments to the original lender. The 2 percent of $782.40 is withheld in case Joe pays off his loan in advance. If this happens, the lender doesn't make what it expected to on the loan, and the dealership forfeits some or all of the 2 percent as its portion of the profits (interest) never made. Remember, the dealership didn't actually lend the money; it simply sold it. In fact, the dealership also gets the check for the $10,000 from the lender, because it was loaned so that Joe could buy his car from the dealer.

There's not really anything fundamentally wrong with the way this works. After all, it's the same way banks make their money. It's only when you add the ever-present elements of deception and greed that this system opens up a wide range of possibilities.

Let's look at a new twist using the same loan amount for Joe and the same buy rate for the dealership. Now you'll see why the question "So how much do you want your payments to be?" is so dangerous.

Once again, Joe has agreed to purchase a car. This time however, when he begins to discuss financing, the dealership's loan officer asks the million dollar question — "So, Joe, how much do you want your payments to be?" or something to that effect. Joe, not fully aware of the impact of his answer, responds with "Oh, I'd like to keep them under $260 a month if I can." Remember that Joe's payments at the 8.75 percent rate of our previous example worked out to be $206.37 per month.

What do you suppose the finance person will do for Joe now? Why, he'll oblige him, of course. The finance person will simply enter the desired payment amount (usually something very close to Joe's limit) into his computer and

Financing, or "How Much . . ."

voilà, wouldn't you know it, "Guess what Joe, the payments work out to be $258.03 a month!" Of course Joe doesn't realize he's going to be paying $51.66 more each month than he would have if he'd done his homework.

The finance person could have given Joe the loan for any amount over the 6 percent buy rate. But since Joe was kind enough to walk into his trap, he set Joe up with a loan at a rate of 18.75 percent. The finance person *raised* the interest rate until it *forced* the payments to come very close to what Joe wanted to pay. So it wouldn't be too obvious, the finance man cleverly made the payments slightly less than Joe's figure, in addition to making sure the payment amount didn't come out too even.

Now Joe will be paying a total of $15,481.80 over the life of the loan, whereas the dealership buy rate meant that the dealer would have paid a total of $11,599.80 to borrow the same amount of money! The result is a whopping $3,882.00 profit to the dealer on the loan itself, not counting the money it made on the sale of the car! Unbelievable. But you better believe it. It happens all the time. *Unless the dealer's lender places constraints on the rate the dealer can charge the customer, the dealership is limited only by the legal maximum interest rate at any given time.* I actually have seen people walk out of a car dealership with a 21 percent (the limit at the time) loan when they could have borrowed the money for 9.5 percent!

If you missed what happened here, I'll explain how it works. Using a computer, the finance person can calculate a loan based on different information. For instance, given the amount of the loan, the length of the loan, and the interest rate, the computer calculates the amount of the monthly payments. On the other hand, given the amount of

The *Only* Way to Buy a Car

the loan, the length of the loan, and the *amount of the monthly payment*, the computer calculates the interest rate. In other words, the computer supplies the missing information so that the dealership can quickly calculate a loan to match the amount you're willing to pay, even if the amount is far greater than what is really needed to pay for the car with a fair profit on the loan. Essentially Joe has just *given away* several thousand dollars more than necessary to the dealership.

So when you answer the deadly question and your payment figure causes the interest rate on his computer to shoot to the moon, well, it's as though Mr. Finance just hit three cherries on a slot machine! Just like the price of the car, the interest rate on a loan obtained through a dealership is a negotiable item. As a rule, however, I would limit my contact with the dealership business office as much possible. It's very easy for an unsuspecting customer to get burned.

The only way to be safe from this threat is to shop around for the best rates on car loans. Historically, credit unions offer the lowest rates. Call a few banks and credit unions to see what they are charging for car loans. They generally don't play the game the dealerships do, and they charge the same rates to everyone. You can call dealerships too, but you'll find it difficult to get them to quote a firm interest rate. Once you've read this chapter, the reasons should be obvious.

Profit is one reason dealers want you to do business with their finance office. Another more subtle but no less important reason is that dealers want you to sign papers immediately after you've agreed to buy a car. You see, they want to finalize the deal before you have a chance to leave the dealership and talk to anyone about what you've done.

Financing, or "How Much..."

A dealership doesn't want a friend or family member pointing out some shortcoming in the deal, and convincing you to cancel and buy the vehicle elsewhere.

■ Rebates and the Rebate or Low Finance Rate Option

The rebate is a relatively modern concept as far as car buying goes. Of course, no one objects to getting money back after a purchase. But why not just make matters simple and lower the price of the car? No. That would be too easy.

The concept of the rebate is simple enough. Buy the product, and the manufacturer will give you back a check for a certain amount of money. You then can subtract the rebate amount from the selling price of the product to figure out exactly what you paid. But that would be just a little too neat and clean for the automobile business now, wouldn't it? Remember: *Anytime there is confusion, or an opportunity to create confusion, there is an opportunity for the dealership to mislead or deceive and, consequently, an opportunity for it to take (not make) more money.*

The fact that you can apply a rebate toward the purchase of a car seems to make sense, right? But to do so, there needs to be a method of assigning the money to the dealership without you having to first cash a check from the manufacturer and then pass the money back to the dealer. It *would* be pretty senseless to have to go through all that. What these wonderful car people have done . . . for your convenience . . . is create a neat little inconspicuous form that does just that. Sometimes these forms are so inconspicuous they resemble a flyer you might find stuffed in your morning newspaper.

The *Only* Way to Buy a Car

Now most of us aren't very fond of paperwork. And if you've ever purchased a new vehicle, you know there are quite a few forms for you to sign when you finally go to pick up your new car. It can be very confusing in all of the excitement. Therein lies the opportunity for the dealership.

It's not uncommon for customers to be completely unaware that a rebate even exists for the model they are buying. In fact, once *I* nearly forgot to ask when I was buying a new car. Strange that the salesperson didn't mention it though. I mean, rebates are supposed to be an incentive for the customer to buy a car, aren't they? I'm sure by now you can see where this is going.

If the subject of a rebate doesn't come up in the process of the customer's buying a car, it's very unlikely that the salesperson will mention it. The hope is that in the confusion and barrage of paperwork on the day the customer picks up the car, the customer unknowingly will sign the rebate back to the dealership. You'd be surprised how often this happens.

Automobile rebate assignment forms usually have two spaces where the customer can sign. Sign in one space, and the rebate is yours. Sign in the other, and the rebate is the dealer's. Many customers are just so glad to be picking up their car that they simply don't read any of the forms but just sign where the salesperson tells them to sign. *It's true!* C'mon, can't you just see it? The customer is high with anticipation, and the salesperson has him or her engaged in a rapid-fire conversation about how great the new car looks or some other such thing. All the while he's shoving forms one after another under the customer's nose for a signature. "We need a signature here, yup, right there, and another one here." Without even knowing it, the customer has just

Financing, or "How Much..."

handed the dealership another $200 to $1,500 for absolutely nothing!

You may be reading this thinking that the customers of whom I speak are the exception or just aren't too bright. Let me assure you this is not the case. Customers who have been unwitting participants in these scams come from all walks of life and levels of intelligence. The success of these tactics depends entirely on some form of deception or purposeful misleading. But then that's really the essence of a scam, isn't it?

There is nothing wrong with a rebate per se. Be sure to ask if there is one and treat it as cash toward the purchase of the car. Any other treatment just increases the chance of confusion. Oh, and, make sure to examine every form before you sign it!

■ The Either/Or Rebate-Low Finance Rate Option

This one basically boils down to a simple math problem. But first a generalization: *Unless you are absolutely certain you're going to keep the car for the full length of the loan, the rebate is always the better choice.*

Here's an example. You've decided to buy a car, and you're given the choice of taking a $1,000 rebate now or getting a low interest rate on a loan for a period of thirty-six months. Let's just say the savings on the loan would work out to exactly $1,000 should you keep the car for the full thirty-six months. Let's assume you take the loan option. It's easy to see, then, that if you decide to get rid of the car before the thirty-six months are up, you won't really have saved the full $1,000 on the financing option. This is be

The *Only* Way to Buy a Car

cause the $1,000 savings has been spread over the length of the loan in the form of reduced payments. If you don't make all of the payments, you don't get all of the savings. Therefore it's better to take the money up front in the form of a rebate. Even if you did keep the car, we could make the argument in favor of the rebate simply because you get the savings now. Time really *is* money when it comes to financing and interest rates.

The rebate option and the loan option seldom work out to be exactly equal in terms of the amount of money saved. This is because the amount of money financed varies depending on your down payment, the price of the car, and so on. If you know you're going to keep the car for at least as long as the loan, then it becomes a simple math problem.

First you have to compare the *total* amount of money you would pay over the life of two different loans. One is the loan you would get from the dealer if you take the low finance rate option; the other, the loan you could get from a credit union, bank, or some other *trustworthy* source. You need to factor in a second loan because if you take the rebate, you won't be getting the low-rate dealer loan. Remember, it's one or the other. *Note:* Readers with computers may have a program that can calculate loans or a calculator that computes loan payment information. Otherwise, you can obtain loan information from your bank.

So let's suppose you're going to buy a car, and the dealer gives you the choice (dealer's choice, there's that gambling metaphor again) of a $1,000 rebate or 4 percent financing for thirty-six months. Assume you'll have to borrow $10,000. Also assume you can borrow from the bank at 8.5 percent for thirty-six months. What to do?

Let's break it down like an accountant would (I used to be an accountant, but don't tell anyone, please):

Financing, or "How Much..."

Loan Comparison	Loan A	Loan B
Amount borrowed	$10,000	$10,000
Loan terms	36 mos @ 4.0%	36 mos @ 8.5%
Monthly payment	$295.24	$315.68
Number of payments	× 36	× 36
Total of all payments	$10,628.64	$11,364.48

Obviously Loan A taken by itself is more attractive. But we need to factor in the other element, the $1,000 rebate. To figure out which is the best option, we have to know what the difference would be if we took the rebate and Loan B. To do this, we simply subtract the total payments under Loan A from the total payments under Loan B ($11,364.48 minus $10,628.64). The answer is $735.84.

So while your total payments are going up by $735.84 when you take Loan B and the rebate, you also are getting $1,000 in cash handed to you by the dealer. More simple math proves that you're actually ahead by $264.16 ($1,000 minus $735.84) if you take the rebate and Loan B!

We could make this exercise more complicated by factoring in the amount of interest you'd earn on the $735.84 in saved payments if you took Loan A, but the amount is too small to be worth the effort. I apologize to you finance purists out there.

Chapter Summary

- Financing vehicles is a very lucrative activity for automobile dealerships. They make their money on loans by charging the customer a higher interest rate to borrow the money than a bank or credit company would charge

The *Only* Way to Buy a Car

the dealership to borrow the same amount. The dealership's rate is known as its *buy rate*. But the dealership itself isn't loaning the customer the money; it's simply *selling* the money for a bank or credit grantor.
- There's nothing inherently wrong with this system. In fact, it's exactly how banks make money, except they actually do loan their customers money and generally establish a fixed rate all borrowers pay on a given day.
- Most people don't realize that dealerships are *selling* money, and so many don't realize that the interest rate, like the price of a vehicle, is negotiable and that dealerships are inclined to charge you the highest rate they can get away with.
- The question "How much do you want your payments to be?" is a trap for unsuspecting customers. Don't answer this question! Just stick to known quantities — the length of the loan, the interest rate, the amount borrowed — and tell the dealership you'll consider financing with it if it can compete with your credit union or bank.
- If a dealership is serious about wanting you to finance with it, make certain you're told up front exactly what the terms of the loan are with respect to the length of the loan, the amount borrowed, the interest rate, the monthly payment, and the total amount you'll be paying over the life of the loan. Be absolutely clear on all of these before you sign! It's lack of information that makes you vulnerable to all dishonest dealership practices!
- If you're going to finance your new car, shop for the best interest rate by checking as many lenders' rates as you can. Credit unions have a history of offering good rates for all types of loans. Even if you do decide to borrow

Financing, or "How Much..."

through the dealer, you'll have a good feel for what you should be paying for an interest rate.

- When you're evaluating the choice between a rebate and a low finance rate, always choose the rebate if you're not sure you're going to keep the car for the full length of the loan. If you know you're going to keep the car, find out the difference in the total of all payments between the low-finance-rate loan and the best loan of equal length you can get if you decide to take the rebate. Then subtract this difference from the amount of the rebate (if the rebate is large enough). If the answer is zero or greater, you should take the rebate.

4

Aftershock... uh, I Mean... Aftersell

Aftersell? What is aftersell? Ah, just when you thought it was safe to walk out of the dealership.

Let me preface this brief chapter with bit of car-buying gospel: *From the moment you walk through the door of a dealership until the moment you leave, the dealer is selling you.* By selling you, of course, I mean that you are the target of a continuous concerted sales effort. You are being sold on the environment at the dealership, a vehicle, the trustworthiness of your salesperson, the quality and level of service, and so on.

For car dealers, these efforts ideally would amount to something of a seduction. You're supposed to be so enchanted with all these things that you'll agree to virtually anything. And I've seen people agreeing to some pretty strange things. Take the gentlemen who handed me a $500 deposit *after* his new car was bought and paid for. Naturally, we accepted it. Or how about the poor guy I mentioned in Chapter 3, the one we stuck with the 21

The *Only* Way to Buy a Car

percent loan? He was one of my customers too. No, I'm not proud of it. Somewhat ashamed, to be honest.

Oh yes, aftersell. I almost forgot. *Aftersell* is the selling after the selling, the selling after the sale . . . after the sale of the vehicle, that is.

If you've read the chapter on financing, you now know that car dealers sell at least one other thing besides cars — money. And they sell lots of other things too. All of these come under the general category of aftersell. As opposed to beforesell, I guess. Lousy joke, I know.

Aftersell is the effort to sell you any number of other products and services once you've been sold a vehicle. This honor usually belongs to your friendly F&I person, the finance and insurance person.

Here's a list of some, but by no means all, aftersell products:

- Life, accident, disability, and other forms of insurance, outwardly for the purpose of protecting you (and yours) from the financial hardship of the automobile loan you've just been saddled with, should you become unable to pay.
- Rust proofing, paint sealers, waxes, ornaments, floor mats, and the like.
- After-the-fact air conditioning, cruise control, sun roofs, and so on.
- Burglar alarms and various other forms of theft deterrents.
- Oh, and of course, what would aftersell be without the flagship aftersell product of them all — the extended service contract (as it's politely being called these days), also known as the dreaded *extended warranty*. (I can hear the dogs howling now!)

Aftershock... uh, I Mean... Aftersell

Aftersell is every bit as dangerous to the customer as financing. And just like financing, every item for sale during the aftersell is negotiable. A successful aftersell session can turn a lousy deal for the dealership into a great one!

One of the reasons aftersell (and financing) has been so profitable for car dealers is that customers often believe the selling is over once they've agreed to purchase a car. They couldn't be more wrong. It's only just begun.

Another reason has to do with your perceptions. Everyone distrusts car salespeople, right? Their character is so stereotyped by now that if your grandmother sold cars, you probably wouldn't trust her.

Well, the F&I person uses all of that negative imagery and stereotyping to help create his own credibility.* He makes a deliberate effort to be perceived differently from a salesperson.

Even his office usually is set up away from the showroom floor traffic. And there's his title — Business Manager (or something close). Obviously, the F&I person isn't part of the sales effort. After all, he's just seeing to the business of how you're going to pay for your car. No threat here. Why, it's like working with a banker, and bankers are pretty trustworthy...

Don't believe it. *The F&I person is a salesperson just like all of the other salespersons at the dealership, only he has more power to hurt you.*

The business office is the ideal setting for the aftersell. You're relieved about finishing the car-buying ordeal. You're relaxed; your guard is down. This makes you a ripe

---

* For simplicity, I've chosen to use *he, him,* and *his* when referring to the finance person in this section, but that person could very well be a *she* or *her.*

The *Only* Way to Buy a Car

target for the F&I person, who already has the added factor of perceived credibility in his corner.

One of the other great hazards of the aftersell is the seemingly painless way in which you can add the purchases made during the aftersell directly to your monthly loan payment. "After all," the F&I person will say, "what's another ten dollars a month?" Another $10 a month over a sixty-month loan is $600, that's what. Frequently he'll quote these additional amounts on a weekly basis to further lessen their impact. For example, "What's another two dollars and fifty cents a week? You spend that much for the morning newspaper."

But the biggest danger facing the customer in the aftersell is simple lack of knowledge, lack of knowledge that the price of aftersell items is limited only to the amount the dealership is able to get you to pay for them, and that most aftersell items can be purchased for much less somewhere else. (See Chapter 6 for a discussion on "ding stickers" and the example of the customer who insisted on having T-roofs installed.)

Let's look at some of the specific items the customer frequently is asked to buy during the aftersell.

Life, accident and health, and disability insurance. And you thought you were shopping for a car. You certainly weren't expecting a trip to the insurance agent. Okay, so you may have overextended yourself somewhat by buying this car. The idea of financial ruin may seem very realistic to you at this time. But is that any reason to overextend yourself more? The insurance offered during the aftersell is geared specifically to covering only your car loan in the event you become sick, injured, or perhaps even die while you still owe money on the loan. As with all aftersell items,

Aftershock . . . uh, I Mean . . . Aftersell

it is generally not a bargain. Here's what Don McEwen has to say:

> I could convince anybody as to why they need life and accident and health insurance. . . . It's a percentage of the monthly payment. Accident and health insurance is much more risk for the insurance company . . . it's provided by an independent insurance company, therefore the premium is higher than the life insurance. The life insurance is, on ten thousand dollars, three or four dollars a month. The accident and health insurance is about eight or nine dollars a month.
>
> You need to read those contracts. There's a sick, injured, or disabled. There's usually a thirty-day elimination period that means they won't make the first payment, but they make all subsequent payments. There's a lot required [on the part of the insured person]. Some insurance companies say that if you can't work at your current vocation, after one year of being out, you have to get some kind of work that you can do. If you don't, they won't pay for it.
>
> The fact of the matter is, a lot of people have good disability plans with their job. The thing they have to understand, though, is that if they are disabled, whatever their disability at work . . . it isn't usually going to cover it [specifically, the car loan]. So disability in some cases is a good policy to have.

Perhaps so. But I would first make sure to check the coverage provided by any disability insurance you already have. And if you do want to have disability insurance geared specifically toward covering your automobile loan,

The *Only* Way to Buy a Car

why not try to buy it from your own insurance agent? You probably can save a lot of money.

Here are more telling comments from Don:

> The life insurance, you can buy term life for about one-tenth . . . you can buy a term life policy on a *hundred thousand dollars* for less than *half* of what you would pay for life insurance on one of these particular loans.

What he's saying is, if you buy your insurance elsewhere, you can buy $100,000 of coverage for *half* the amount you would pay at a car dealership to cover a typical car loan!

Rust proofing, paint sealers, waxes, ornaments, floor mats, air conditioning, cruise control, sun roofs, burglar alarms, and the like. Depending on the practice of the dealership, these items are sold as aftersell or appear on what's known as an addendum or "ding sticker" that's attached to the vehicle window. (We look at the ding sticker in some length in Chapter 6.) The items that appear on the ding sticker are for the salesperson to sell before you enter the office of the F&I person. Regardless of who is responsible for trying to sell them, most of the items can be purchased outside of the dealership for considerably less money. And some of the items are of questionable or dubious value. As with any add-on, the sky is the limit in terms of what you will be charged at the dealership.

All manufacturers now offer some sort of rust-through warranty with their new vehicles. The typical coverage is five years or 100,000 miles, whichever comes first. Even in the most hostile climates, you seldom see rust on a vehicle

Aftershock... uh, I Mean... Aftersell

less than five years old. Before manufacturers' warranties, there may have been a need for additional rust proofing, but I don't feel it's necessary now.

My only comment with respect to the more tangible vehicle add-ons is to shop around. You virtually are assured of being able to buy these items at a specialty shop for far less than you will pay at a dealership.

The extended warranty or extended service contract. These contracts can extend the types and length of warranty coverage that automatically comes with the purchase of a new car. Don McEwen makes a solid case for two possible situations in which a customer would be a good candidate for a contract of this sort.

- The customer is young or a recent graduate and has limited financial resources, or, I suppose, it could be anyone working with a very tight budget. The purchase of a new vehicle has put a considerable strain on this person's resources, so much so that the need for a major repair could place the individual in serious financial jeopardy.
- The customer travels extensively for long distances using the car or vehicle.

In the first case, it's easy to see how shifting the repair cost to the manufacturer with an extended warranty could be a lifesaver. The wisdom of getting yourself in debt to this extent is questionable to begin with though.

The second case offers the driver the comfort of knowing that the car could be repaired at any dealership that sells the brand of car being driven. No criticism from me on that one. If you've ever had to have repairs done at an unfamiliar garage, you know how nerve wracking it can be.

The *Only* Way to Buy a Car

Don McEwen makes an additional, excellent point: The customer should consider buying an extended service contract only from the manufacturer of the vehicle. Third-party warranties may not be honored where you need to have your car repaired. (Another nightmare!)

The extended service contract or warranty, like everything else, is negotiable. *Watch out*. Widespread abuse of warranty sales has led some lenders to limit the amount a customer can add to a vehicle loan to pay for a warranty. But that doesn't limit the amount the dealership can charge you if you're paying for the contract out of pocket. According to Don McEwen, extended service contracts are marked up 200 percent to 500 percent and more.

Chapter Summary

- Aftersell is the attempt by dealership personnel to sell you additional products once you've agreed to purchase a car. Aftersell is usually the responsibility of the person who handles the business and paperwork end of the car purchase — the F&I manager or the business manager.
- Like financing, aftersell is a virtual minefield for the unsuspecting customer. Among the reasons for this are the following:

    √ As much as possible the F&I person separates himself from salespeople. Customers generally are not aware that selling takes place in the business office, so they tend to trust the F&I person more than they should.
    √ The customer tends to relax once the decision to buy the car has been made.

Aftershock ... uh, I Mean ... Aftersell

√ It's easy to include the cost of aftersell products in the amount the customer is financing because these products tend to add incrementally small dollar amounts to monthly payments.

√ The price of most aftersell items usually is wide open, something most customers don't realize. The selling point of these products is the small monthly payment. No one mentions what may very well be an astronomical price for the item.

- Nearly all aftersell items can be purchased at places other than the dealership for less money. Before you decide to buy insurance, a sunroof, or any other aftersell item from the dealership, be sure to shop around. *And* make sure you know the total price of the item you're buying, not just the amount that's going to be added to your monthly payment.
- If you have to purchase an extended warranty, consider only those offered by the manufacturer of the vehicle. And remember, warranty prices are negotiable too, that they're typically marked up 200 percent to 500 percent. Begin negotiations for the warranty by offering the dealership one-quarter to one-third the amount it asks for. Be persistent. It would rather sell you one at a small profit than not sell you one at all.

5

To Lease or Not to Lease

Leasing a vehicle has become a popular alternative to an outright purchase for many people these days. In a way, a lease nicely fits our need for immediate gratification. Being the practical person I am though (and I'm assuming you're pretty practical too . . . after all, you're reading this book), I'm not sure I see much sense in it.

You see, I am a shopper. There, I've said it. True confessions. Now, I'm not one of those shoppers who will nickel and dime someone to death; nor will I drive 50 miles to save $2 on an item. But my shopping philosophy is to buy things for the least amount of money possible. Vanity plays absolutely no role in my buying decisions. In other words, the chance of me buying something to impress my neighbors is roughly equivalent to that of my mother enlisting in the Marines. And I'm not inclined to make impulse purchases. In the terms of the marketing professional, I'm what's known as a *laggard*.

And what does all this have to do with leasing a vehicle? Simply this: *If you lease a vehicle, you almost always will end up paying more profit than you would if you*

The *Only* Way to Buy a Car

buy the vehicle. And that alone is contrary to everything this book is about.

Paying more in profits is less offensive to some people than others, so let's take a look at how a lease works.

■ "How Much Do You Want Your Monthly Payments to Be?" — the Leasing Version

What *is* this obsession with monthly payments anyway? For one thing, it seems like you can buy virtually anything and pay for it monthly these days. For another, many people have bought (literally) into this credit system so heavily that the monthly payment is the only basis they have for figuring out if they can afford to buy something.

The monthly payment is one of the big selling points of a lease. Because you are not buying the car outright, monthly lease payments can be substantially less than monthly purchase payments.

In practical terms, a lease is nothing more than a long-term rental. A car lease is very much like a lease for an apartment or piece of property. You use the property during the period the lease is in effect; and when it's over, you return the property to its owner. Under most vehicle leases, you are responsible for insurance, maintenance, and repairs — as you would be if you owned the car.

When you contract for an automobile lease, you usually are contracting with a third-party leasing company, not the car dealership. In other words, you actually are leasing the vehicle from a company other than the dealership. The dealership merely functions as the middleman in the deal.

This is how it works: The dealership has a business relationship with one or more leasing companies. These com-

To Lease or Not to Lease

panies give the dealer formulas and lease plans with which the dealer determines the amount of the monthly payments and the other terms of the lease — the length of the lease, the number of miles the vehicle can be driven over the term of the lease, and either the customer purchase option price or the method by which the value of the vehicle will be determined at the end of the lease.

A typical lease term is between thirty-six and forty-eight months but can be more or less. The number of miles allowed is a strict lease condition: The customer must pay a penalty — usually 10 to 15 cents per mile — for each mile driven over the limit. The purchase option price is exactly what it sounds like — the price for which the lease customer can buy the car at the end of the lease.

Unless you're the type of customer salespeople fondly refer to as a *laydown* (that is, a sucker, someone who's ready to pay a huge amount of money for a car), a dealership would much rather have you lease a car than buy one. The reason for this is simple: profits.

You know that car buyers seldom pay a dealership full sticker price for a new vehicle. But remember that a lease contract is usually between the customer (the lessee) and a third-party leasing company (the lessor). How is it that a third party can make a contract for a car the dealership owns? It doesn't. First it *buys* the vehicle from the dealership. Right before your very eyes.

That's right. The dealership actually is selling the car to the leasing company and handling the paperwork for the lease agreement between *you* and the leasing company at the same time. What difference does that make? None if you're one of the strict-monthly-payment types I described earlier. But it makes a big difference if you don't want to give the dealership any more profit than you need to.

The *Only* Way to Buy a Car

To learn more about leasing, I spoke with John Witte (pronounced *witty*), sales manager for Lundgren Honda in Auburn, Massachusetts. Here John talks about the transaction in which the leasing company buys the car from the dealership:

> The customer's credit, and their employment, their income, that type of thing, can play a factor. ... Different lease companies have different guidelines. Some lease companies will advance [pay the dealership] up to the sticker price of the car. Some lease companies will advance *over* the sticker price of the car.

This is indeed a very nice arrangement for the car dealership. Given the right circumstances, it's possible the dealership actually could receive *more* than the sticker price for the car from a leasing company. There are very few customers who would agree to those terms if they were buying the car. So why should they agree to them when they are leasing?

Maybe I should explain. If the leasing company is paying in excess of the sticker price for a car, who is going to pay the leasing company? The lease customer, of course!

Now, I don't mean to imply that the leasing company always or even frequently pays more than the sticker price for a car. But it is possible. Once again, it's the good old monthly payment at work. Consider these comments by John Witte:

> At this point in time, and I think that in the future this may change, at this point in time, the lease agreement doesn't have what they call a *cap*

To Lease or Not to Lease

cost disclosure. The cap cost is what the customer is actually paying for the car. That would be the selling price. If it was a cash transaction or a conventional finance loan, that's all disclosed obviously to the customer.

In the lease, the only thing that the customer is furnished with are the lease payments and the terms, that type of thing. So, in some cases, the dealership is able to hold . . . possibly a better gross profit than they would in a conventional finance deal, simply because the customer, all they see is the savings that they're getting on a monthly basis, and overall as far as the cash out-of-pocket is concerned. So the selling price isn't the issue in a lease. It's the terms and the payments and that type of thing.

I would imagine that some point in time down the road, that the government will require some type of a cap cost disclosure on a lease agreement so the customer knows what the lease payments are based on. But right now that isn't the case.

Call me stupid, but I could swear that this means lease customers have no idea what they are paying for the car! And that the law doesn't even require that they be told! Now, are you sure you still want to lease that car? If you do, I've got a great house you can buy too. Your monthly payments are just $1,500 for the next fifty years. No, no, I have no idea how much it's going to cost, but it's just $1,500 a month.

Let me point out one more bit of irony peculiar to this business of leasing. Look back at what John Witte had to say on page 56. Notice that he indicates that the customer's

The *Only* Way to Buy a Car

credit quality is a factor in determining the price at which the vehicle is sold to the *leasing company*. It may not be obvious at first, but this means that a customer with poorer credit actually can wind up paying *less* for a lease than a customer with better credit! Why? Because the customer with better credit can *afford* to pay more profit, so, of course, he or she *will* pay more profit. Isn't that beautiful? As they say, only in America.

■ The Anatomy of a Lease

Lease payments are based on several components. First are the obvious elements: the length of the lease and the mileage allowance. Usually a lease term is between thirty-six and forty-eight months, and a lease usually allows the car to be driven 15,000 miles per year. Beyond these basics are the cap cost element and what is known as the *money factor*. In addition, residual value (the value of the vehicle when the lease is up) is a consideration in figuring out the amount of the lease payments. Two other factors — the acquisition fee and the disposition fee — also play a part in determining the cost elements of a lease.

- The *cap cost* is the actual price paid for the car by the leasing company.
- The *money factor* is similar to the spread between the buy rate paid by the dealership and the interest rate a customer pays in a conventional finance loan when purchasing a car. It's the difference between what a leasing company has to pay to borrow money to pay for a car and the rate it charges a lease customer to tie up that money in a lease.

To Lease or Not to Lease

- The *residual value* is the value of the vehicle to the leasing company at the end of the lease. It is subtracted from the beginning value (cap cost) of the car to determine how much of the value of the car is being used up in the course of the lease.
- The *acquisition fee* is a charge — typically $400 to $500 — that's built into the lease payments as profit for the leasing company (according to John Witte).
- The *disposition fee*, usually an amount less than the acquisition fee, is charged to the customer supposedly to cover the costs of such things as the paperwork associated with terminating the lease.

So, to explain in a very rough, inexact way, lease payments are calculated like this: The leasing company takes the price it has paid the dealership for the car (the cap cost), which already includes a healthy profit to the dealer, and adds its own profit on top of that. It then adds a profit for the money factor (the amount of profit you are going to pay to tie up the company's money in the car). From this figure, it subtracts the residual value (what it believes the vehicle will be worth at the end of the lease). Once more, it adds in an amount for the acquisition fee. All that remains, then, is to divide the total into monthly payments over the life of the lease. Of course, at the end of the lease, you will pay the disposition fee. Remember, I said this was a rough explanation. But you get the idea.

Now I don't begrudge the leasing company, the dealership, or anyone else for that matter the right to make a profit. But likewise, I don't begrudge the customer the right to try to avoid paying profits either. And there are clearly ample profits to be avoided in a lease. But how?

The best way to avoid paying profits in a lease is simply

The *Only* Way to Buy a Car

not to lease at all. Your only other defense is to have the dealer reveal the cap cost to you and to try to negotiate it down to a lower amount. In addition, if you can choose a leasing company, choose the one with terms best suited to your budget.

■ The Great Debate

Let's take a look at some of the arguments dealerships make in favor of leasing and respond to each.

- *"You avoid having to come up with a large down payment with a lease."* This is generally true. However, most leases require the first month's lease payment up front along with one month's payment as a security deposit. Some leases, in fact, do require a down payment, usually called a *cap cost reduction*. Besides, a vehicle often can be purchased these days with little or no down payment.
- *"You avoid having to pay all of those sales taxes up front with a lease."* The key words here are *up front*. You still have to pay sales taxes, but they are figured in as part of each monthly payment.
- *"Your monthly payments can be much less with a lease."* This generally is true, depending on the length of the lease. But where is your money going? To profits, fees, and the like. You are simply paying to use the car; you're not earning any equity.
- *"Why buy something you know will be worth half of what you paid a few years from now?"* Why rent something for approximately the same money you could be buying it for? Suppose you take a loan of $12,000 to buy a car.

To Lease or Not to Lease

Even at an interest rate of 10 percent for forty-eight months — with a monthly payment of just over $300 ($304.35 to be exact) — more than $200 ($204.35) of your *first* payment actually is going toward paying for the car itself. And *more* of each subsequent payment. If you have a lease payment of $300, you're paying $300 in interest, fees, and profits, on top of paying for someone else's car. When the lease is done, you have nothing but paying a disposition fee to look forward to. When you're done paying for the car you bought, you'll have a vehicle worth several thousand dollars. Somebody is paying for the car that's been leased, and that somebody is the customer. If you're going to pay for it, you might as well own it. And if you play your cards right, you probably will pay a hell of a lot less profit to buy a car than you would to lease it.

- *"You can drive a nicer car for the same monthly payment."* Potentially true, but you're still not going to own it. See the arguments above.

The only conditions under which I recommend that someone lease a car are these:

- You absolutely need a brand-new car, and either you don't have enough money for a down payment or you can't qualify for a no-money-down purchase.
- You have money to burn, and you don't object to paying a hefty profit and not owning the car once you've finished paying.

The *Only* Way to Buy a Car

Chapter Summary

- Leasing has become popular because little is required in the way of a down payment and because monthly payments are generally less than they would be to purchase an equivalent vehicle.
- This emphasis on down payments and monthly payments is not without a price though. The fact is that with most leases, you're paying far more in fees and profits than you would in a typical purchase situation. In the process, you're paying for someone else's vehicle too.
- You still pay sales taxes when you lease if your state requires them — they are just added in to each lease payment.
- Lease payments are calculated roughly like this: The leasing company takes the cap cost (which already includes a healthy profit to the dealer) and adds its own profit on top of that. It then adds a profit for the money factor — the amount you pay the leasing company to tie up its money in the car. From this figure, it subtracts the residual value — what it believes the vehicle will be worth at the end of the lease. Then it adds an amount for the acquisition fee (more profits). All that remains is to divide the total into monthly payments over the life of the lease. Of course, at the end of the lease, you will pay the disposition fee.
- The fact that many vehicles can be purchased today with little or no down payment makes the case in favor of leasing much weaker than it once may have been. The only conditions under which I recommend that someone lease a car are these:

To Lease or Not to Lease

√ You absolutely need a brand-new car, and either you don't have enough money for a down payment or you cannot qualify for a no-money-down purchase.

√ You have money to burn and you don't object to paying a hefty profit and not owning the car once you've finished paying for it.

6

D-Day or Mayday?

So the big day is about to arrive. Time to go baffle 'em with your brilliance. That shouldn't be too hard.

You now know more about car buying than 99 percent of all consumers and perhaps a good percentage of car people themselves. And you definitely know more than car people want you to know! But we're not finished yet. Almost, but not quite. You need a few final bits of knowledge to propel you into the ranks of true car-buying superstars!

I've chosen "D-Day or Mayday?" for the title of this chapter because these words respectively are symbols of victory and defeat. The extent to which you put into practice what you've learned here will determine whether your trip to the dealership winds up a D-Day or a Mayday.

First we talk about determining the dealer's cost for the car you want; then we look at what's going to take place at the dealership.

The *Only* Way to Buy a Car

■ Determining the Dealer's Cost for Your New Vehicle

For a new vehicle, there is really only one way to determine the dealer's cost: Get the information from an impartial third party. Some dealers will show you their invoice, but I think you may have noticed that I have *zero* faith in any information provided by a dealership or its agents.

Two of my favorite sources are *Consumer Reports* magazine's car price service and a book called *Edmund's New Car Prices*. For less than $10, the *Consumer Reports* service will send or fax you a report that shows you the dealer's cost for the exact model car you are looking for, including an item-by-item breakdown of options exactly as they appear on the sticker. This report is worth every cent. For even less money, the *Edmund's New Car Prices* book shows the same information for almost all current makes and models. It is available in most bookstores.

Here are numbers for the Consumer Reports service:

Voice phone: (914) 378-2000
Fax: (313) 347-2985

A credit card is required for an immediate response.

Once you've obtained one of these sources, to determine the dealer's total cost, simply add the dealer's cost for the base price of the car and any optional equipment included on the car you are considering.

The only adjustment to this cost information that may be necessary is for an advertising allowance if your dealer belongs to a local or regional advertising group. Dealerships from the same area selling the same brand of cars sometimes belong to an advertising collective. Each dealer-

D-Day or Mayday?

ship in the group contributes a certain amount of money per vehicle as payment for advertising done on behalf of the entire group. For example, the New England Oldsmobile Dealers Association runs advertising encouraging you to "visit your New England Oldsmobile dealer today."

These costs can run up to $500 per vehicle. It's really up to you to decide if you want to pay them, negotiate them, or find a dealer who doesn't belong to a group.

In addition to the *Consumer Reports* price service and the *Edmund's New Car Prices* book, a number of other publications and organizations offer similar information. For example, the AAA Automobile Club offers this service to its members, as do some oil companies if you happen to be a holder of their credit card. My experience with *Consumer Reports* has been so good, though, that admittedly I'm partial to the price service.

If you are considering buying a used car, then you already know how to determine dealer's cost or thereabouts. You'll want the ACV of the used car (see Chapter 2).

One final word on the topic of dealer's cost: It is impossible to know the exact final cost to the dealer for any given new vehicle. Why? Because of factory-to-dealer programs that are, as the name suggests, arrangements strictly between manufacturers and their dealerships. These are discounts to the dealer that can be based on the sale of a particular model, the sale of a model with certain features, the volume of sales of a particular model, and so on. The discount per vehicle can amount to anywhere from $200 to $2,000 or more, and the programs are usually in effect for a limited time. These programs are strictly off limits as far as the customer is concerned. So just accept the invoice cost as being the closest you will get to knowing true dealer's cost.

The *Only* Way to Buy a Car

■ Reading Between the Lines at the Car Dealership

Typically you're accosted by a salesperson the moment you set foot on a car lot. I say *typically* because, believe it or not, some dealerships are trying a new approach and calling off the dogs. They call it *soft sell*.

Call it soft sell, soft peddling, or even soft serve. I don't care. Just remember it's only an approach, and it's the enemy. It doesn't matter if a salesperson kisses you or hits you over the head with a two-by-four. It's the substance of the visit you're concerned with, not how it's packaged, right? Right.

Part of any salesperson's success with an approach is the ability to communicate with the customer, to establish a rapport. And communication is a two-way street. I mean, you're not going to have much success if your audience simply doesn't respond, are you?

Two of the salesperson's best tools for opening up communications with the customer are the open-ended question and the alternate advance question.

An *open-ended question* is exactly what it sounds like — a question that requires an answer other than yes or no. Here's an example of how an open-ended question works. You walk into the dealership, and you're approached by a salesperson. Her typical greeting would go something like this: "Hi, what can we help you with today?" Notice that she doesn't ask "Can I help you?" or "Can I help you with something?" If she had, you could have responded with a simple no, creating a very uncomfortable situation for her.

Responding to the first question, though, you're more likely to say something a lot less threatening, such as "Well, we're not sure just yet." Although this might not be the ideal response she's looking for, it's a good deal better

D-Day or Mayday?

than a flat-out no. It doesn't immediately close the door to a conversation with you. And you may even respond by telling her exactly what you're looking for.

The *alternate advance question* requires you to respond with one of two or more choices the salesperson gives you. Naturally these choices are exactly what she wants to hear. If the salesperson asks the question properly, there is no bad answer you can give her. Here's an example: "Tell me Joe (substitute your name), are you looking for a family car or something a little sportier?" What are you going to say? No? You'll probably respond with one of the choices you've been given. It's only natural.

Many people unconsciously use this technique in normal conversation. I often hear my wife ask her young son, "So what would you like for lunch, John, a tuna fish sandwich or a peanut butter sandwich?" I've never heard John reply, "Oh, I'll have a ham and Swiss on rye." And I never fail to smile.

To help develop a spirit of agreement with the customer, salespeople will use a third technique, the tie-down. The *tie-down* can be especially annoying if you are aware of it and it is used to excess. It is accomplished by a simple question that confirms or reaffirms something positive that you have just told the salesperson. For example:

You: This is a pretty sharp looking car.
Salesperson: Isn't it though?
You: Yes, it really is.

You: I've seen a lot of these in my neighborhood lately.
Salesperson: There are quite a few of them on the road, aren't there?
You: Oh yeah, you wouldn't believe how many.

The *Only* Way to Buy a Car

You: Boy, my friends would be impressed to see me in one of these!
Salesperson: They sure would, wouldn't they?
You: Yes, they would.

Well, you get the picture. The "isn't it," "aren't there," "wouldn't they," "shouldn't it," or "couldn't it" doesn't always have to appear at the end of the sentence, does it? Oops, sorry. But the idea is to get you to begin unconsciously agreeing with them, even if it's on something as trivial as the weather. Hopefully you'll be agreeing to a not-so-trivial car purchase a little later on.

One last technique worth of mention is what I call the *hot potato*. (Is it *potato* or *potatoe*? Let me check with Dan Quayle.) For the salesperson, the hot potato is especially effective for avoiding a potential deal-killing blunder.

Suppose you've shown strong interest in a vehicle but are somewhat hesitant about moving forward with the purchase. If the salesperson has been effective, you may feel as though your opportunities to escape are dwindling. In an act of desperation, you may look for a way out by stating an objection that you believe will be impossible for the salesperson to overcome. For example: "Gee, you know, I really like this car, but do you have one with a yellow interior?"

If the salesperson answers with a simple no, the deal is as good as dead; and you breathe a sigh of relief and walk out the door. However, the smart salesperson will turn right around and dump the question back in your lap: "Is the yellow interior something you want?" You're now forced to reveal whether this is something you really want or if you were just bluffing. The salesperson always has an answer for a customer's response, and with this particular

D-Day or Mayday?

technique, the customer usually winds up looking like a fool in the process.

So why all of this talk about sales techniques? After all, you're not training to be a salesperson. It's simple. You just need to be aware of where and how the salesperson is trying to lead you every step of the way.

Not only are questions effective tools for opening up the lines of communication; they also are tools of control. Think about it. *The person asking the questions is usually the person who controls the conversation.* The question is the salesperson's fundamental weapon. With each question you answer, you're pointing the salesperson to a certain car on the lot. But, do you want them to tell *you* which car to buy, or would you rather tell *them*?

■ Getting Around Questions and the Whole Approach

Not for one minute do I suggest you enter a dealership with a chip on your shoulder or a defensive attitude toward the salesperson or the process. You need to exercise a little diplomacy. After all, you're going to thwart every effort made to "sell" you.

There are many sales trainers who believe that customers actually *enjoy* being sold. I couldn't disagree with them more strongly. There is a sinking feeling that comes with having been persuaded to do something you have doubts about. Yes, some people find their salesperson entertaining and personable. Fine. But I firmly believe the customer should maintain full control over the car-buying process and should do so without any pressure or manipulation from the dealership.

The *Only* Way to Buy a Car

There are two key things *you* must control before you can control a visit to the dealership. First, and perhaps most important, there are your emotions. They are your worst enemy at a car dealership. So many people give away so much by getting excited about a car in the presence of the salesperson. You *must* remain rational and play the game. To a dealership, a car is only merchandise. Salespeople don't get attached to their vehicles no matter how beautiful they may be. You should at least *act* as though this is the case with you. A great hedge against your emotions is a willingness to choose between two or more different makes and models. Not only does this increase your chances of getting a car you want at the right price, it also gives you more dealership choices in your immediate area.

The second thing you need to control is camaraderie with the salesperson. The simplest way to do this is to maintain a businesslike attitude, to put a lid on the small talk and joking around. This doesn't mean you should be hostile. But it *is* possible that you are going to spend a sizable sum of money, and that's a decision worthy of your full attention. Besides, I've known salespersons who would fleece their friends and family without blinking an eye. In fact, I know a salesperson who actually ripped off his mother! No kidding. Another "gentleman" looked forward with relish to a biannual visit from his brother-in-law and a virtually guaranteed big commission.

So then, how do you respond to this barrage of questions? You shouldn't have to. My suggestion is this: Simply walk into the dealership and, when you're approached by a salesperson, exchange a greeting and say: "If you don't mind, I'd like to have the opportunity to look around in privacy for a while. When I'm ready to talk, I'll be happy to

D-Day or Mayday?

look for you. Why don't you give me your card?" Of course you don't have to use these exact words, but I think you can see the beauty of this approach. It's really a win-win situation. You get to wander around the dealership in relative comfort, and the salesperson has a customer who's going to seek him or her out just for having given the customer a card.

My recommendation in Chapter 1 was for you to do most of your shopping away from the dealership. Don't think for a second you'll be able to get a dealership's "best price" for a car by just walking in and asking for it point blank. *The only way to get the best price is to figure out what it is on your own ($100 to $300 over dealer's cost) and to be willing to pay it.* A dealership isn't going to give you a firm price if you're just shopping around. A competitor would simply undercut the price by a few dollars.

For a firsthand look at cars, make your first visit to the dealership when it's closed. If you've followed my advice, you should be able to limit the time spent (and consequently the amount of things that can go wrong) at the dealership to a minimum. With me present, my aunt bought a brand new car in a matter of five minutes at the dealership! We were actually there for fifteen minutes, but ten of those minutes were spent doing paperwork and discussing payment and registration arrangements. Oh, and she got a terrific deal! And the salesman was happy too!

■ You're in Control

This portrayal of car dealerships and salespersons has clearly demonstrated the opposing positions of the buyer and the seller of the vehicle. We've examined the tech-

The *Only* Way to Buy a Car

niques and tricks used by sellers. We've illustrated how each and every word out of the seller's mouth is spoken with just two purposes in mind: To get customers to buy a vehicle during their first visit and to have each customer pay as much as possible for that vehicle.

Let me sum up, in a general way, my strategy for approaching a trip to the dealership. Essentially it boils down to this: A visit to the dealership is nothing more than a game. The best thing for you to do is not to play the game at all. You don't have to be rude, just don't play. It's *your money*, so *you* should control the outcome. If you know what you want and how much you're willing to pay, just go in there and buy it! Dealership personnel may make every effort (including lying) to sidetrack you and get you to play the game. Don't bother. If you play their game, you're going to lose. Go in there and make an offer to buy the car. If they don't like it, *leave*. Your ability to say no is one of your greatest strengths. The dealership down the street *will* sell you the car for your price.

In 1988 I decided to buy a new car for myself. Now I wanted this particular car *very* badly. None of my local dealers was being a good sport about selling me the car I wanted for the price I wanted to pay. But I didn't get ruffled and run out and pay their price. I went shopping. I wound up buying the car at a dealership 250 miles away, for $1,500 less than anyone would sell it to me for in my local area. This is an extreme example, I know, but it only cost me $89 to fly there and pick it up. And my local dealers were obligated to provide the manufacturer's warranty service.

Before you walk into the dealership, you should know exactly

D-Day or Mayday?

- which car you want to buy with which options.
- the dealer's cost of the car you want to buy.
- how much your present car is worth (ACV) if you're trading.
- how you're going to pay for the new car.
- how much you're going to pay for the new car.
- the amount of the rebate, if any, on the new car.

Negotiating should be virtually unnecessary. You may want to be somewhat flexible in your offer, but just a little bit. Say $100 at the most.

■ Stickers, Stickers, and More Stickers

The law requires that at least one sticker be present on a new car. That is the Monroney sticker, and it's placed on the car by the manufacturer.

The Monroney sticker can be identified by its large size and the presence of the manufacturer's logo. It lists the location of the manufacturing facility and the dealer to whom the vehicle originally was shipped; it also lists the base price of the vehicle and prices for individual as well as packaged options. The last figure on the Monroney sticker should be preceded by the words "Total Manufacturer's Suggested Retail Price for Vehicle Including Options" or something like that.

You should be able to match the options on the Monroney sticker exactly with those on your *Consumer Reports* cost sheet or in the *Edmund's New Car Prices* book. This is important. If you can't, you probably are not looking at the Monroney sticker.

The *Only* Way to Buy a Car

The Monroney sticker is the only sticker you should use to determine the list price of the car. It's almost absurd that I have to to explain how to get the list price, but it shows just how hard the industry has worked to confuse the customer. Remember, in confusion lies opportunity for the dealer.

Many dealerships practice the sneaky habit of putting their own stickers on their cars in *addition* to the Monroney sticker. These are known as *addendum stickers,* or, more fondly, *ding stickers.* When asked about these additional stickers, Don McEwen had this to say: "Well, we call them *ding stickers.* They are commonly referred to in the business as *ding stickers* because you're just going to ding the customer." Clear enough.

It is usually pretty obvious that ding stickers have been placed on the car after the fact. Sometimes they're even handwritten. But others are not nearly so obvious. Some dealers' ding stickers use the same colors and design as the Monroney sticker, which gives them a more official appearance. Another trick is for the dealer is to place the ding sticker so that one of its edges lines up with an edge of the Monroney sticker, which gives the appearance of one, very large sticker.

Some of the items commonly listed on ding stickers include rust proofing, paint protection, and some sort of applied noise deadener. More from Don:

> Every customer has a right, whether I believe in a product or not . . . to decide whether he wants it or not. Some people believe in rust proofing . . . other people say it's useless. That's not up to me to decide. If the customer wants rust proofing, he can

D-Day or Mayday?

buy it. But it's not up to me to *give* him, whether he wants it or not. It creates a hostile environment right off the bat with the customer.

"What, the presence of a ding sticker?" I asked.

"Absolutely, absolutely," replied Don. "If you went in to buy lunch and somebody threw dessert at you and said you had to take it, it comes with it, and it costs five dollars more and you can't get the lunch without it, you'd be upset. It's the exact same thing."

Although the products listed on ding stickers may exist, the prices you're asked to pay for them amount to nothing short of highway robbery. They generally are not endorsed or applied by the manufacturer, and they do not come with the vehicle when shipped from the manufacturer. To put it bluntly, they are simply put there (along with the ding sticker itself) to increase the dealer's profit margin.

Very occasionally a ding sticker actually lists a tangible add-on, something like a false convertible top or perhaps a fin on the back of the car. Cars with these extras usually are kept inside the showroom to grab your attention. Don McEwen explains that frequently dealers modify a vehicle this way hoping that if customers do not necessarily purchase that particular vehicle, they may want to purchase some of the same add-ons for the vehicle they eventually do buy.

My general advice with respect to ding stickers: *Ignore them.* Don't even let talk of the ding sticker or its components into your discussions with the dealer or salesperson. If the car you're considering is equipped with one or more of the tangible add-ons I've described, I suggest you select another model with only factory-installed equipment. Many of

The *Only* Way to Buy a Car

these add-ons are available from outside companies, often for far less money. In fact, dealers often send their cars out to have this work performed.

One of my own customers insisted on having glass T-roofs installed on his new car. This add-on increased the price of the car by $2,000. However, it cost the dealership only $900 to have the installation done at a company specializing in this sort of thing. This company also performed this type of work for retail customers, and it was located nearby, so the customer could have taken the car there himself and saved $1,100!

Often salespeople will insist on including the ding sticker amount in the price used as the starting point for your negotiations, even if you have demonstrated your awareness that it's a scam. Their rationale goes something like this: "Yeah, I know it's just a bunch of bull, but what do you care what the starting price is? You only care about the bottom line, right?" Well, if it's just a bunch of bull, why even talk about it? Just ignore the ding sticker(s) and refuse to discuss it. The only purpose it serves is to confuse you, and we know where that can lead.

In the next chapter, you'll learn how to avoid talk about ding stickers and every other irrelevant thing. It describes a direct and effective method of accomplishing the business of buying a car.

Chapter Summary

- Information is the key to a successful visit to a car dealership. One of the most important pieces of information you need is the dealer's cost for the vehicle you want to buy. Two very good sources for dealer's cost information

D-Day or Mayday?

are the *Consumer Reports* car price service and the *Edmund's New Car Prices* book. You'll have to pay for this information, but it's worth every penny.
- Add up the cost figures for the base price of the vehicle, and any options *actually present on the vehicle you are considering*.
- You may choose to adjust the cost information you get to include an amount for advertising if your dealer belongs to a regional advertising group. If the dealer is inflexible about these advertising costs and you don't want to pay them, go elsewhere.
- Use the ACV as the dealer's cost if you're considering buying a used vehicle.
- Salespeople use questions as one of their fundamental tools when they try to sell you a car. By asking you the right questions, salespeople can develop a rapport with you and get you to reveal important information that helps point them to the car *they* want you to buy.
- Watch for open-ended questions, alternate advance questions ("Would you like a two-door or a four-door?"), the tie-down ("isn't it?" "shouldn't it?" "couldn't it?"), and the hot potato.
- My best advice is to dismiss the salesperson politely once you've entered the car dealership. Simply say that you want to wander around in privacy and promise to speak with him or her once you are ready to do business. By doing this, you don't have to play the question-and-answer game, a game that's designed to let the dealership win.
- Before you go to the dealership to actually buy your new vehicle, you should know the following:

    √ Which car you want to buy with which options

The *Only* Way to Buy a Car

- √ The dealer's cost of the car you want to buy
- √ How much your present car is worth (ACV) if you're trading
- √ How you're going to pay for the new car
- √ How much you're going to pay for the new car
- √ The amount of the rebate, if any, on the new car

• Ignore all stickers on the new car other than the official Monroney sticker. If the car has a tangible add-on (perhaps a rear fin or false convertible top) listed on a ding sticker, my suggestion is to buy another vehicle with manufacturer-only equipment. You can add add-ons later, at a company that specializes in them, usually for a lot less money.

7

How to Buy a Car

Armed with all the necessary information, you're ready to buy the car . . . provided, of course, that the dealer has the car you're looking for. Just a few comments on this subject.

You have a number of choices if the dealer does not have the vehicle you want to buy in stock:

- Go elsewhere.
- Order the car you want from the manufacturer through the dealer.
- Have the dealer try to locate your car at another dealer and arrange for a swap.
- Compromise and buy a vehicle with slightly different equipment or features.

Under no circumstances should you give the dealer any money to try and locate a car at another dealership for you. There is little if any expense involved in a dealer's getting on the computer and looking at another dealer's inventory. You may want to give the dealer a conditional deposit, *if* you agree on price *and* the dealer is going to bring the car

The *Only* Way to Buy a Car

to the dealership. Who knows? The car may have a problem you won't discover until you actually inspect it.

If you decide to order a vehicle from the manufacturer, a deposit is appropriate. A check for $250 should suffice.

Okay. Back to the deal. Assuming the car you want is available, walk into the dealership and dispense with the salesperson as I've suggested . . . but not before finding out where the vehicle you want to see is located. Inspect the vehicle for any physical defects (much easier to do in the daytime). If you want to take a test drive, retrieve your salesperson (you have his or her card, remember?) and do so. No need to engage in any idle question-and-answer games. Perhaps for a little role-reversal fun, you might want to try bombarding the salesperson with open-ended questions. Check the mileage and make sure the car is not a demo (a demonstration model). If you buy a demo, you're nuts! Most demos are driven mercilessly by salespeople. You can get every bit as good a deal on a nondemo.

Having completed the preliminaries, you enter the showroom and sit down with your salesperson. He or she asks you fifty times if you like the car. You say yes. Let's say you've figured out beforehand that the cost of the car plus $100 comes out to $17,000. Now is your moment in the sun. You confidently state, *"I'll buy the car right now* for seventeen thousand dollars." Period. Not another word. Depending on the make, model, and dealer, exotic cars (Ferraris, Porsches, and the like, although there's no harm in trying!) excluded, you may have to go as high as $300 over cost. But not a penny more. Absolutely hold the line at $300. For a domestic car, luxury or not, I would hold the line at $100.

Under any circumstances, *do not* give the salesperson a

How to Buy a Car

deposit before your offer is accepted. Often, in an attempt to force you to stay and negotiate, the salesperson will ask you for a deposit to "let my manager know this is a serious offer." It's not necessary, so don't buy it. The magic words in your offer indicate how serious you are.

The only thing a deposit with an offer accomplishes is to force you to play games until you can convince dealership personnel you want to leave and that your deposit had better be returned. I've actually witnessed customers wait an hour to have their deposit returned, when the dealership knew all along that it wasn't even close to a deal. Some customers were forced to come back another day!

The entire negotiation should take no more than five minutes. You're looking for a simple yes or no. If the answer is no, thank the salesperson for his or her time, walk out the door, and don't look back. Don't hang around and listen to the sob stories. (You'll have a chance to hear those sob stories in a couple of days, when the salesperson calls you on the phone.) A competitor *will* sell you the car for your price.

The bottom line is this: Offer $100 over cost to buy the car right then and there. It's almost as if birds start chirping in their head when they hear the magic words "I'll buy the car right now."

Some publications suggest negotiating the price of options separately from the base price of the vehicle. For what reason? So you can wind up paying more for the car? Your goal is to give the dealer as little profit as possible on the total vehicle. There's no sense complicating things.

It's common knowledge that car dealers will accept between $100 and $300 profit on the sale of a new car. But they are not going to offer to do so right off the bat. The

The *Only* Way to Buy a Car

methods I've described here are the simplest way to get the vehicle you want for the price you want. Follow them and you won't be disappointed!

Unfortunately, there is no hard-and-fast rule to determine the amount you should be willing to pay over dealer cost for a used vehicle. Because warranty requirements for a used car vary with the age and mileage of the car, the risk to the dealer that something could go wrong with it during the warranty period varies as well. But used cars typically have a much higher markup than do new vehicles. The minimum markup is generally in the vicinity of $1,500 and can be as much as $4,000 or more! Personally, I would limit the amount of profit I'd give to a dealer on a used vehicle to $500.

■ A Word on Negotiating

No matter how prepared you are for your visit to the dealership, situations occasionally arise that require you to negotiate. Try to avoid negotiating altogether. But if you must, here are some things to remember:

- You always have the option of saying no to whatever it is you're negotiating for. This is one of your greatest strengths at a car dealership, which would much rather sell you *something* than nothing at all.
- In any negotiations, there's a great deal of psychological game playing going on. It's very easy to be bluffed by someone at a dealership because every employee there supports the dealership's position and you're playing on their field.

How to Buy a Car

- It's always to your advantage to begin with a very low offer. Usually neither of the negotiating parties gets exactly what it wants. So if you start with an offer below what you're willing to pay, you're more likely to end up paying something close to the amount you want. It takes a lot more effort for a salesperson to drag you up several hundred dollars than one or two hundred dollars. Oh yes. The salesperson is going to act offended, insulted, amused, or hysterical; and he or she is going to try to make you feel like a real jerk for having made such a low offer. But don't fall for it. *Make them work for every dollar they get from you.*
- One of car dealers' negotiating tricks is to come down in price by very small increments. For example, you may be looking for the dealer to knock several hundred dollars off its price in one step, but instead it makes a first drop of $50. It can get very discouraging and have you second-guessing whether you actually can buy the car for the amount you thought you could. Don't believe it! It's only a game, and you can play too. If you're going to raise *your* offer, raise it by $10! That's right, $10. The next time, raise it by $5.

Chapter Summary

- Visually inspect the vehicle at the dealership and take a test drive if you want. If the car meets with your satisfaction, sit down with your salesperson and make your offer: the dealer's cost for the car plus $100. You may want to go as high as $300 over cost, but no more.
- Never give a salesperson a deposit before your offer is

The *Only* Way to Buy a Car

accepted. You don't need to give a deposit to show that you're serious. Just tell them, "I'll buy the car right now for $_____ ." That's as serious as you need to get.
- Don't negotiate optional items separately. Make your offer for $100 to $300 over the *total cost* (base price plus the cost of options). Negotiating for options is asking for trouble.
- If the dealership refuses to sell you the car for the price you're offering, go somewhere else. You *will* find a dealership that will accept your offer.
- There is no set amount of lowest profit a dealer will accept for a used car. Start by offering an amount as close to the ACV of the car as you can. My advice is to not pay any more than $500 above the ACV.
- Avoid negotiating if possible. And remember, you can always say no and walk away.
- Negotiating involves a lot of psychological game playing, and you're at a tremendous disadvantage because you're playing on the dealership's field.
- Start negotiations with a very low offer and increase it only by small amounts. Make the dealership work for every dollar it gets.
- And remember: Every day is a sale day at the car dealership! Good luck.

Car-Buying Worksheet

Use this worksheet to calculate the amount you will offer the dealership for the new vehicle you want to buy. Unless you are planning to order from the manufacturer, fill in the items as they appear on a vehicle the dealer has in stock.

Make and model of the new car: _____

Dealer's cost of Monroney sticker
base price of vehicle: $_____

Options and dealer's cost for each:

_____ $_____

_____ $_____

_____ $_____

_____ $_____

_____ $_____

_____ $_____

The *Only* Way to Buy a Car

Total dealer's costs
(base price plus options) $_____

Subtract: Actual cash value (ACV)
of your trade in   ($_____)

Total amount needed
for dealer to break even
($0 profit, dealer invoice) $_____

Add: $100 profit $_____100_____

Total amount of your
offer to buy new car
(in addition to your trade-in) $_____

Glossary of CarSpeak

For your amusement, I've included this list of some of the colorful and derogatory terms commonly used by people in the retail car business, along with their meanings.

All the money	Getting customers to pay top dollar, or giving customers full value for their trade-in ("We're giving her all the money").

Bump	An upward step in money obtained from the customer ("If I bump him $300, we'll have a deal") or a switch to some other product. ("He was looking at the truck, but I bumped him over to the Lemming").

Buried	Over one's head in debt; owing far more for a car than it's worth.

Card	Invoice price. ("We'll sell you the car for $200 over card").

Deuce	$200.

Dirtbag	A person of low social standing; a person who doesn't have the money or credit to buy a vehicle.

Do re mi	Money.

The *Only* Way to Buy a Car

Downstroke	Down payment.
Flake	A customer who walks away from a deal after agreeing to buy a car.
Get bought	Be approved for financing by the dealer's lender. ("Can he get bought?" or "Can we get her bought?"). Implied meaning: Can the customer obtain financing for the amount he or she needs to borrow to buy a *specific* vehicle?
G note	$1,000.
Grape	An unintelligent, slow person.
G whiz	G note.
Home run	Same as "all the money." Implies a big commission.
Laydown	A customer who's very easily sold.
Mind deal	A sale that is never going to materialize.
Nickel	$500.
Over the curb	The car has been delivered to the customer.
Quarter	$250.
Spiff	An incentive to the salesperson (usually money) to sell a certain model vehicle. Usually paid by the manufacturer or the dealer in addition to ordinary commission.
Stiff	A person with bad credit.

Glossary of CarSpeak

Stroker A person who has no intention of buying, who's just wasting the salesperson's time.

Tissue Invoice price.

Toilet A car in bad condition or of poor quality.

Two bucks $200. The same goes for three bucks, four bucks, and so on.

Upside down Owing more money for a car than it's worth.